THE THIRD WORLD

☐ Africa

☐ East Asia

☐ Latin America

☐ Middle East

■ South Asia

☐ Southeast Asia

THE THIRD WORLD

SOUTH ASIA

Author
JAMES NORTON

Editorial Director
DONALD K. SWEARER

Pendulum Press, Inc.
West Haven, Connecticut

ISBN 0-88301-059-3 Complete Set
     0-88301-064-X This Volume

Library of Congress Catalog Card Number 72-92907

Published by
Pendulum Press, Inc.
The Academic Building
Saw Mill Road
West Haven, Connecticut 06516

Printed in the United States of America

Cover Design by Ampersand Ltd.

CONTENTS

ABOUT THE AUTHOR

James Norton received the B.A. and M.A. degrees from Oxford University, an M.S. from Yale University, and a PH.D. from the University of Madraf in India. After teaching for five years at the University of Madurai in India, Mr. Norton returned to the United States where he has taught at the College of Worcester, Boston University and is currently at Oberlin College.

FOREWORD

THE THIRD WORLD has been written to provide much needed materials on non-Western cultures. In the past, most studies of the non-Western world were chronological in organization or dealt with the regions studied by using the traditional themes of religion, politics, history, and so on. Very few, if any, offered the student a thematic perspective.

THE THIRD WORLD discusses the regions of Africa, East Asia, Latin America, Middle East, South Asia, and Southeast Asia from the perspective of societies and cultures in transition. This has been done in a variety of ways: by focusing on the problems of new nations struggling with the issues of economic development; by organizing the study around the major minorities of a region; by investigating the ways in which traditional norms and modern forms interact; and by seeing the problems of modern non-American cultures in the light of the anxieties, conflicts, and tensions of our own society.

In their own ways, the authors of each of the volumes have attempted to make their regions come alive. Each author teaches subjects related to the region about which he has written, and all have spent considerable time there. Consequently, they have a feel for the peoples and the cultures.

The authors of the volumes of THE THIRD WORLD are not only interested in these countries from an academic point of view. They also hope to be able to make a contribution to world understanding and world peace by increasing your knowledge of non-Western cultures, peoples, and societies.

THE THIRD WORLD has, in short, been written with a sense of urgency and a sense of mission. The urgency is the chaotic state of today's world. The mission is knowledge, not the kind of knowledge that comes from memorizing facts, but the understanding that comes from dispelling myths and from grappling with problems relevant to you and the world in which you live. You have a stake in the future of the world. It's a rapidly shrinking world in which the problems of the Third World are your problems. It's up to you to try to solve them. We hope that THE THIRD WORLD will be of some help along the way.

—**Donald K. Swearer**

I. INDIA: A PLACE, A CIVILIZATION, AND A PEOPLE

When thinking of India, many images come to mind. India is poor, overpopulated, burdened with more than its share of disease and natural calamities. India is an ancient, exotic land, a holy place. India is an elephant, large and cumbersome. To those who know it well, the elephant has dignity, grace, and a quiet disposition. It also has a will of its own that must be respected.

How can we describe this land of contrasts, where ancient and modern, rich and poor, weak and strong live side by side and often mix together?

India is first of all a place. For many centuries the name has generally designated a distinct region along the southern rim of Asia. This area, which projects more than a thousand miles into the Indian Ocean, is clearly set off from the rest of Asia by the high Himalayan Range. This mountainous wall, some eight hundred miles long, has over twenty peaks above twenty-four thousand feet. Mt. Everest (29,324 feet), the highest mountain in the world, is in this range. Isolated on all sides by mountains and ocean, this South Asian region is easy to identify on a topographical map.

When the British relinquished their Indian Empire in 1947, India became the largest of eight nations which now occupy the area known as South Asia. Their political boundaries have not usually followed the geographi-

cal divisions. Ceylon is the only country in South Asia
with a completely natural boundary. The exact boundaries of India are still in dispute with its most extensive
neighbors, Pakistan and China. The unsettled division
of Kashmir, between India and Pakistan, and the dramatic incursion of Chinese forces into India in 1962, reveal the continuing tension along these borders.

India is a large country, approximately 1,260,000
square miles, about one-third the size of the United States.
A closer look at the topographical map on page 11 reveals five distinct geographical regions within India. The
northern Himalayan region, rising abruptly out of the
plain, caps the subcontinent. The region is sparsely populated because of its steeply rising slopes. Large tea estates
occupy the foothills of Assam in the east. Shepherds graze
their flocks of sheep and goats in the high valleys of the
central and western regions. Sherpa traders trek through
the high mountain passes. Less frequently, holy mendi-
cants seek the heavenly serenity of the mythical Mount
Kailasa.

The northern plains, south of this Himalayan range,
form the second geographical region. Three great river
systems provide the plains with a constant flow of melted
snow: the Indus, curving around the western end of the
Himalayas; the Jumna-Ganges, flowing down the southern slopes and eastward through the Gangetic plain; and
the Brahmaputra, curving around the eastern end to the
Bay of Bengal. These plains are the most fertile and the
most densely populated section of India, holding about
66 percent of the population. The settlements are mostly
rural and small. At the lower end of the Gangetic plain
the population density rises to an average of one thousand
inhabitants per square mile. Most of the people are dependent upon agricultural produce, although many neither

own nor work the soil.

Rising between the southern edges of the Indus and Gangetic plains are the Thar desert and the rugged hills of Rajasthan. This area constitutes part of the third geographical region of India. These hills are the northern end of an older, smaller range called the Western Ghats which extend in increasing height to nine thousand feet toward the southern tip of India. Although less precipitous than the slopes of the Himalayas, these mountains are also sparsely populated. The rugged hills of the north have long been associated with military and romantic heroism of the Rajput and Maratha princes. In the more remote reaches of the south are coffee and tea plantations, shelter for wild game, and some of India's numerous tribal populations.

East of the Western Ghats is the fourth region, Deccan, a central, peninsular plateau. During the monsoon rains, June through August, the Western Ghats become the source of the plateau's most important rivers: the Godavari, the Krishna, and the Kauvery. The Deccan, like the northern Gangetic plain, is composed of small, agrarian villages. But the people of this region have their own customs and traditions because of geographical and linguistic separation from the north. Only during the times of great empires has it shared in a common political history with the Gangetic plain.

Between the mountainous rim of the Deccan plateau and the surrounding ocean waters is the coastal region: the Malabar Coast on the west and the Coromandel on the east. These narrow strips are the most tropical, providing luxurient growth during the monsoon seasons, particularly along the densely populated southwestern shore. Here the population in some areas rises to four thousand per square mile, the highest rural density in India. Three of India's largest cities are located in the coastal region: Calcutta, Bombay, and Madras. All were started as ports of commerce by the British East India Company in the seventeenth century and became modern urban centers under British rule. Only the ancient capital city of Delhi, which became the capital of British India in 1912 and remains the capital of independent India, is comparable in size. Its 1971 population of 3.6 million ranks it with the coastal cities: 7 million in Calcutta, 5.9 million in Bombay, and 2.5 million in Madras.

The clear delineation of the physical outline of the South Asian subcontinent identifies India as a particular geographical area—an area of vivid contrasts in altitudes, temperatures, rainfall, and the diverse activities, customs, and densities in population. But India is more than a region or place. India is a civilization, one of the most distinctive and ancient in the world.

Popular images of India, of Maharajas riding on elephants or cobras weaving to the tune of a snake charmer, have now given way to more sophisticated images. Its poverty, heightened by the recent horde of refugees from East Bengal; its artistic achievement, demonstrated in the sitar performances of Ravi Shankar, and its mystical thought and meditation—all portray India as a distinct culture. It is a civilization with its own patterns of expression and achievement.

During the time of American discovery and exploration, India was considered a land of incredible wealth. The magnificent splendor of the Moghul, Rajput, and Vijayanagar kings and the finery of their courts and palaces lured European explorers during the sixteenth century. Their quest for Indian riches gave the name Indian to America's own native population, a name based more on the explorers' hopes than on what they found. India's wealth, however, has been its achievement as a civilization. Its cultural refinement distinguishes India from other civilizations and affirms the unique integrity and contributions of its people.

Characteristics which identify the evolution of distinctive Indian culture began around 2700 B.C., with the construction of two major cities, Harappa and Mohenjo Daro, 350 miles apart in the Indus River valley in northwestern India. The origin of this ancient urban culture is unknown and presents an intriguing puzzle. For these two cities are among the earliest known to man. With their broad main streets, large granaries, and intricate drainage systems, the builders brought to their contruction an understanding of the needs of urban life. The cities appeared suddenly, fully developed. They flourished with amazing consistency for one thousand years. Mohenjo Daro was rebuilt seven times during this period, but each time according to the same plan as the one before it.

The inhabitants of these cities developed active trade with the emerging civilizations in the Mesopotamian valley to the west. Yet, they remained untouched by the technological advances of the Bronze Age, until they were destroyed around 1700 B.C., as suddenly and mysteriously as they began. The existence of this urban culture remained unknown until 1922, when archeologists began to unearth their hidden artifacts and reveal their remarkable achievements. Still only partially understood, what has been reconstructed gives tantalizing suggestions of their continuing impact on the development of India.

The development of the priesthood among the Aryan tribes which invaded the Indus valley around 1500 B.C., may have its origin in this urban culture. Even today, suggestions of the Harappan heritage can be seen in the images and worship of the important Hindu god, Shiva.

And the rupee, India's primary unit of currency (about 13.5¢), was divided into sixteen units called annas. This one to sixteen proportion of measure was uniformly applied in the ancient city of Harappa over 4,500 years ago.

This Harappan culture is the earliest known of India's many heritages. Following it, we find a series of traditions which fall into these general historical periods:

Harappan	2700 - 1700 B.C.
Aryan - Vedic	1500 - 500 B.C.
Buddhist	500 B.C. - 300 A.D.
Mauryan	324 B.C. - 183 B.C.
Kushan	50 - 150 A.D.
Classical Hindu	300 - 1000 A.D.
Gupta	320 - 467 A.D.
Medieval Islamic	1000 - 1857 A.D.
Delhi Sultanate	1206 - 1398 A.D.
Moghul	1526 - 1707 A.D.
British Colonial	1756 - 1947
Independent	1947 -

All of these periods have contributed to the complex patterns of Indian thought, customs, and social interaction. As a place, India is the location of an ancient, intricate, and intriguing evolution of life styles.

But even more essentially, India is a people. Its large population of over 550 million, one-seventh of the world's total and almost three times that of the United States, is in size alone a significant segment of mankind. Not all Indians live on the Asian subcontinent. There are Indian communities as far away as Trinidad and the Fiji Islands. Everywhere they express the distinctive characteristics of their culture. But the Indian people also share with all of us the diversity, complexity, and unpredictability of being human.

This study intends to communicate the vitality of India as a place, a civilization, and a people, focusing on different aspects of Indian life today.

First, we will examine India through two aspects of modernization—economic and political development. Thus, in Chapter II, we will describe India's development toward a self-sustaining industrial economy, like those of the United States and Japan. By this measure India is considered a poor yet developing country. In Chapter III, we will discuss India as a modern political state, having a constituted, stable, representative government. By using these two descriptions we can identify India's problems and progress in the process of modernization.

The economic and political structures describe India on a national level. Another level of activity in Indian life today is the village. Because the vast majority of India's people live in villages the dynamics of the village provide the basic social context for many changes which are taking place. Therefore, in Chapter IV, we will describe a traditional village social structure, called the *jati* caste system. In Chapter V, we will see how the process of modernization has affected and is affected by this traditional structure.

Another aspect of Indian life is its classical tradition. This tradition is still a primary force in village life, particularly in religious practices. It is important to recognize it and to distinguish its more abstract patterns from the practical, down-to-earth reality of the village. In Chapter VI, we will describe Hindu religion on the village level. And in Chapter VII, we will contrast the village *jati* caste system and the *varna* caste scale, described in classical literature.

In the final Chapter we will discuss the classical tra-

Clemens Kalischer

These radiant faces typify the exotic beauty of the Indian people.

dition as it relates to India as a modern nation, for like the village social structure, the classical tradition also provides a framework toward understanding India's emergence as a modern nation. The coming together of the classical and modern, in the person of Mahatma Gandhi, the founder of India's independence is a particularly striking example. Through his leadership, India was able to discover and express a life-style appropriate for these times and yet consistent with India's history as a distinct human culture. These descriptions of the village, of caste and religion, and of Gandhi's leadership and genius will give us a basis for understanding India today.

The aim of this study is to encourage such understanding, challenging enough to involve us and profound enough to arouse in us a deeper appreciation of India's people. This study will make us more aware of their circumstances, their problems, and their aspirations. To meet the challenges which face our nation today, we must have a more sensitive and informed response to the perspectives and concerns of peoples around the world.

Our aim, therefore, is not to tell you what you should know about India, but to encourage you to become responsive to its people. Together we have a vital opportunity to discover as yet uncharted constellations in our common universe as men.

QUESTIONS FOR DISCUSSION

1. Some people have suggested that the distinctive cultures of Europe, China, and India can be identified with the "personalities" of their rivers: the turbulent, purposeful, forceful Rhone; the easy, steady, meandering of the Yangtze;

and the alternate devastation by flood and drought of the Indian rivers. Do you feel that the comparisons of cultures with their rivers are either accurate or helpful? Why or why not?

2. The author, on the other hand, feels that the development of culture can be found in what man has done with his environment rather than how the environment has conditioned him. Do you agree? Why?

3. Our thoughts and images about unknown people and cultures are largely shaped by our preconceptions. What ideas come to mind when India is mentioned? List them and discuss as a class. Do you and your classmates agree on your picture of India. If so, how do you account for this agreement. Are there common sources and what are they? If there are differences among your classmates on their images of India, how would you account for this?

II. ECONOMIC DEVELOPMENT IN MODERN INDIA

The Indian subcontinent has been involved in the process of modernization for over a century. But even with such long experience, a self-sustaining economy has not developed in any of the present nations in this part of the world. Nor has the political potential been consolidated beyond a point where even its strongest nation, India, can take more than a moral stance in international affairs. It does not have enough political or economic power to enforce its national interests in the world. As a modern nation, it is a weak though independent country.

During the period of British rule in South Asia, many of the important preconditions of a developed, self-sustaining economy were begun. An extensive network of railroads and highways (a necessary element to industrialization) was constructed during the nineteenth century with British capital. Irrigation works undertaken during this period provided India at the turn of the century with the second highest amount of acreage under irrigation in the world. And British administrators struggled impressively with recurring droughts and famines.

A comprehensive, if exclusive, system of education was developed, consistent with the policy adopted in 1835, to educate an Indian elite in the English curriculum. Three major universities were established in 1857 (in Bombay, Calcutta, and Madras), to provide for the administrative, professional, and business needs of a modernizing colony. By 1947, there were nineteen such institutions across India, offering degrees in medicine, law, engineering, the sciences, and the arts.

And yet, this base was far from adequate because of the immense size of India and the counter objectives and preoccupations of England during the twentieth century. In 1947, only 2 percent of the labor force and 6 percent of the national income were provided by the industrial sector of the economy. With over 80 percent of the population living in rural areas, agriculture was by far the greater source of employment and income. And over 27 percent of the active agricultural working force was employed for less than an average of ten days per month. When employed, these landless laborers received the equivalent of only about 14½¢ a day. With such a low, subsistence level of economic activity and such a high rate of unemployment and underemployment, the per capita income in 1947, was less than $50 per year, one of the lowest in the world. It was hardly a firm basis upon which to build a thriving, self-sustaining economy.

India's record since Independence in 1947, has been impressive in many ways. Prime Minister Jawaharlal Nehru undertook economic development as a top priority for the government. In 1951, the first of a series of Five Year Plans was instituted to allocate public and foreign aid resources to stimulate economic growth. Four such plans have been drawn up by the highly competent and politically insulated Economic Planning Commission, covering the period up to the present.

In the industrial sector, these plans have concentrated primarily upon the heavy, basic industries. These industries provide such things as petroleum, electric power, metalurgical materials, and chemicals for other industries which provide employment and products. With such stimulation, many of these industries have increased substantially. Steel production has risen six times from 1.5 million tons in 1950 to 9 million in 1970, and more than six times as much electricity is being generated over the same period. (2.3 kilowatt hours in 1951 to 14.3 in 1971.) In these specific areas, India's economy has improved and gives promise for continuing growth and expansion.

In the agricultural sector, the planning emphasis has been on technological improvement and social reform as the most effective means of increasing food production. Great gains have been made in agricultural technology, particularly in the development and increasing use of hybrid seeds and artificial fertilizers. Annual food grain production has almost doubled over the past twenty years, from fifty-four million tons to over 105 in 1970. With such a tremendous rate of increase, this "green revolution" achieved self-sufficiency in grain production in 1972.

But in terms of the overall impact, India's advance toward a self-sustaining economy is more promise than reality. Over the past twenty years, the average per capita income has increased by little more than $1 per year, leaving India still near the bottom of the list of the world's poor. Spectacular as some changes have been, particularly in technological advances in agriculture, development efforts have not been large or effective enough to overcome the immense obstacles to rapid expansion needed to achieve the take-off point to a self-sustaining economy.

Agricultural development, more effective land distribution and water use are essential, although it is difficult to see how they might be accomplished when rainfall is erratic and unpredictable. Also, political and social power remain in the hands of those who manage agricultural production. Their effective control in rural areas has

Farmers work their fields with the aid of ox-drawn plows.

Clemens Kalischer

contributed to the failure of cooperative farming and land distribution programs. Land redistribution itself does not meet the most immediate problems: underemployment and low productivity per acre.

More effective changes in the purely economic sphere should result through greater coordination between agriculture and industry. Crops could be turned into cash to supply raw material for industry. Food processing plants, farm equipment plants, and fertilizer manufacture would provide less seasonal forms of rural employment and an increase in productivity and income. The investment capital needed to begin such coordinated development is scarce, both in India and from international sources. And the necessary spirit of enterprise and initiative is hard to sustain when so much of a cultivator's effort is required simply to provide for the needs of his family.

Other factors have contributed to India's economic stagnation, and some are totally beyond India's control. The international monetary situation, for example, has not favored developing countries. The average increase in per capita income during the 1960s in developed countries was $650. Among less privileged nations, the increase for the same period was less than $40 per person. In India, the brief but expensive war with Pakistan in 1965, followed by extensive drought in the lower Gangetic Plain in 1966 and 1967, put severe strains on the economy. These caused major disruptions in the third Five Year Plan and delayed further growth.

During the summer of 1971, millions of refugees poured across the border from East Bengal to escape the repression of the West Pakistan military government. In great masses they arrived, at a rate of up to thirty thousand per day, weary, frightened, and helpless people with few personal belongings. By the end of October, their number was estimated close to ten million. Most were barely surviving in squalid, crowded refugee camps along the borders. This influx placed a tremendous burden on India's already meagre resources, calling for vast expenditures for a humanitarian need.

The immense strain placed on India by these refugees only underlines the extent of its own population problem. Because of the rapid growth of its population, India is barely able to provide for its own people. A population of 361 million in 1951, has risen an average of about 2.4 percent per year to 547 million in 1971. It continues to grow at a rate of over one million per month, or with an additional Indian to feed and clothe about every 2½ seconds.

The population growth has been so close to the increase in industrial and agricultural production that what has been gained in more food, jobs, and income has simply been absorbed by the increasing numbers. This factor alone largely accounts for the slow change in the per capita income. Thus without some effective means of slowing the population increase, a significant gain in India's national economy is difficult to imagine.

The difficulty of stemming this population increase is immense. People want to have children. And for people who are poor, children provide the only source of pleasure and security that they know. Public supported welfare programs, social security, and medicare exist in few societies in spite of the universal need for such care. In India care is provided only by the family.

It is also important to recognize that the rate of population increase is a result of modernization. The very factors which indicate Indian development—a greater food supply, a slight increase in family income, social reform, and more effective medical care—have contributed to the population increase. In the early years of this century, the population was stable because the birthrate and the death rate were approximately the same: around forty-five births and deaths per thousand population per year. The dramatic change which has taken place since then is not in a rising birthrate. It has fallen to about thirty-nine per thousand. The change is the reduction in the number of deaths, estimated in 1971, to be around fourteen per thousand. People are healthier, better fed, and are living longer. Without these gains, there could be no development in India at all. With them, the population itself becomes a problem.

As the size of the population has increased, the Government of India has taken steps to reduce the birthrate through a national family planning program. This program has sought to bring about a change in attitudes and social practice through education and communication. Yet, its most effective means to date have been technological in character. The most significant results have occurred where there has been the use of birth control devices. But their impact on the total population has not been great.

Even more vital, however, is a change in the social expectations and habits of the people themselves. For the greatest obstacle to family planning is one of information and acceptance. There are few opportunities within the traditional family structure to plan family size, and few assurances that, even when planned, a limit of two children will provide adequately for the family's future needs. Thus population control, as in the case of the development of the economy, cannot be isolated from the traditional social fabric of India as a whole.

These examples of industrial, agricultural, and population change are some of the economic factors which

Children provide a source of pleasure and security to the poor.

Clemens Kalischer

describe India as a developing country. Although exposed to some aspects of a modern, industrial economy, India has not achieved a self-sustaining level of economic growth. For many people, the direction and the increasing pace of development are cause for guarded optimism. India is realizing its economic potential. The increase in agricultural production and the industrial-business activity in the cities lend conviction to this hope.

And yet, India has also advanced to a stage where the people experience the burden as well as some of the fruits of modernization. Many Indian people remain impoverished and underemployed. There are few places in India where this sad condition does not exist.

India is an economically developing country with much human pathos and suffering. Yet the people remain hopeful and the government committed to a policy of planned economic growth.

QUESTIONS FOR DISCUSSION

1. India's industrialization was comparable to Canada's and Japan's in 1900. What factors have kept India's from developing as rapidly as the other two?

2. In what ways, if any, should the United States assist India's economic development? Should United States aid be conditioned upon India's acceptance of United States directives in foreign policy, for example, toward Pakistan, Vietnam, China, or the Soviet Union? Why or why not?

III. THE POLITICAL STRUCTURE
OF MODERN INDIA

To describe India in terms of its economic development is only one measure of its modernization. A different
measure of development is conveyed if we examine India
politically.

When India became independent in 1947, after nearly two hundred years of British colonial rule, the country
emerged with many elements of a stable government. A
representative legislative body, an administrative service,
and an army were all trained in the best tradition of British colonial service. Equally important, there was an effective political party, the Indian National Congress. The
Congress Party was founded in 1887, to involve more Indians in the colonial government. When Mahatma Gandhi became its president during the 1920s, its members
worked effectively to involve the people in the movement
for political independence. On August 15, 1947, the Congress leadership took the reins of government from the
British officially. It had already won the people.

One of India's first tasks was to define itself, as an independent government. This was done through the Constitution, adopted on January 26, 1950, establishing
India as a secular, democratic Republic. The document
itself, directly traceable to the heritage of British rule, incorporated much Western political theory. The Constitution's framers, under the leadership of Dr. B. R. Ambed-

kar, consciously drew upon the American, French, and Irish Constitutions as examples of viable models for a modern state. Its Preamble has a familiar sound. It is the responsibility of the Republic to ensure that all citizens enjoy:

> *Justice,* social, economic, and political; *liberty* of thought, expression, belief, faith and worship; *equality* of status and opportunity; and . . . *fraternity* assuring the dignity of the individual and the unity of the Nation.

The Constitution separated the powers of government into three branches: the legislative, the executive, and the judicial. This is also familiar to us although the relationship between the legislative and executive branches in India follows the British pattern. The initiative and responsibility for leadership rests in Parliament, in the person of the Prime Minister, not with the President. In India, the President is elected by a majority of the legislators, not directly by the electorate. Once elected, the President serves more as a symbolic Head of State than as a political leader. His role, thus severely limited by the Constitution, gives him no authority to determine national policy.

The most important body of the government is the lower of the two houses of Parliament, the *Lok Sabha* (the House of the People). Almost all of its 524 members are democratically chosen representatives of the people, elected for up to five year terms in a national election. All adult citizens are entitled to vote in national elections.

The Prime Minister, the leader of this House, is officially invited by the President to form a ministry, but he must enjoy the support of a majority of the House in order to remain in power. Should the Prime Minister lose a vote of confidence (a provision attached to almost all major legislation), he or she would resign. The President may, if he felt that another member of the Lok Sabha had the support of a majority, invite him to form a government. Otherwise, the President dissolves the Parliament and declares a national election to determine which party has the greatest support of the people. Since the Congress Party has held a majority in the Lok Sabha since Independence, there has never been a vote of no-confidence. Consequently, the issue of who is to be Prime Minister has been determined within the ranks of this Party.

According to the Constitution, there must be a new election before the lapse of five years at which time Parliament is automatically dissolved. Every member must stand for reelection if he wishes to continue in office. This pattern has been the most common. Of the five national elections held since 1952, the first four occurred at five year intervals up to March 1967.

The Prime Minister may, however, ask the President to dissolve Parliament at any time. He may especially wish to do so at a time when an election would appear to be most advantageous to his own leadership. This was the case in December, 1970, when Mrs. Gandhi made such a request; and the fifth national election occurred a year earlier than necessary. While many thought her power waning, her overwhelming victory in this election, proved her political wisdom.

The governments in each of the eighteen States of the Union parallel the national government. The State Legislative Assemblies are composed of democratically elected members for up to five year terms. Each is led by a Chief Minister, appointed by the State Governor, but again dependent upon the will of the majority in the Assembly.

The function of the State Assemblies is significant in

a variety of ways. First of all, the states reflect the political, geographical, and historical circumstances in the formation of the Republic as a whole. Independence did not involve simply the transfer of power from the British Raj to the governments of India and Pakistan. It also meant the incorporation of a large number of autonomous kingdoms—some 40 percent of the subcontinent—which never came under direct British rule.

Incorporation of these autonomous kingdoms involved a number of assurances and compromises. The most important consequence has been the creation of states on the basis of language and religion, highly sensitive issues culturally and politically. The States Reorganization Act of 1956, established the basic pattern of drawing boundaries according to the language spoken by the majority in a region. The subsequent divisions of the old state of Bombay into Maharasthra and Gujurat in 1960, and of East Punjab into Punjab and Harayana in 1967, are further developments of the same pattern. A significant factor in the war between India and West Pakistan in December 1971, is the fact that the people of Bangladesh shared a common language with the Indian State of West Bengal from whom they were politically divided. They did not have such a link with West Pakistan.

Another consequence of the incorporation of many autonomous states into the Republic of India was the delegation of many areas of public concern to the state governments. The State Legislative Assemblies thus have control over a number of subjects designated by the Constitution, concerns such as agriculture, land revenue, health, education, and public order. Policies with respect to two crucial issues in India today, land reform and the language of instruction in schools, have been legislated on the state rather than the national level because of this constitutional provision.

These Assemblies are much closer to the electorate in both impact and sensitivity to local and regional pressure groups. The style of these bodies is therefore quite different, their concerns more regional, and their membership less stable in their allegiance to particular parties and leaders. In many states, Chief Ministers have continued in power with only fragile alliances of many different groups. And they have been forced to resign on no-confidence votes when these alliances crumbled. There have been instances when no alternative leadership has been available. Then a constitutional provision to impose direct rule by the President of the Republic in the State has been exercised. A number of mid-term elections have been held in the states, most notably the so-called mini-election of 1969. Elections were held simultaneously in five different states. A number of opposition parties had joined together for the sole purpose of defeating the Congress Party in 1967. They won the elections, but their alliances were not strong enough to forge a common policy. And so within two years they collapsed, invited President's Rule, and new, state-wide elections were held.

The structure of the Indian government thus is both complex and flexible enough to be workable in this widely diverse and linguistically divided nation. It has provided stability and some sense of purposeful participation for the people of India. The strong leadership of India's first Prime Minister, Jawaharlal Nehru, and now of his daughter, Mrs. Indira Gandhi, has had a great deal to do with this achievement. Both have been committed to the democratic process, but have also appealed to a wide spectrum of support because of their astute political leadership.

The quiet but vital role of the Indian Administrative

Service has also been significant. Recruited by competitive exam from among the best students in the universities, this elite corps of highly trained and dedicated civil servants has provided wisdom and consistency to the government's policies, both as the secretaries to the ministries which formulate the legislation and as the executives who implement it. Their effectiveness has prevented the need for military involvement in the government, a condition which has not existed in many other emerging nations throughout the world.

The role of the political parties, particularly the Congress Party, has been important. As a result of Gandhi's political activity, the Indian National Congress Party mobilized the people and stimulated their participation in the political process. Building on this base since Independence, the Congress Party has become the strongest party. It has combined strong organization, regional flexibility, and a plurality of the popular vote. Because no other party has been able to gain such a national following, its long-standing dominance in national politics has also contributed to India's political stability. Even the major split in the Party which occurred in 1969, has not disrupted its effectiveness in bringing political issues and a sense of national purpose to the people.

To recognize these political achievements is also to underline the problems which India faces in establishing its identity as a nation. Difficulties built into the constitutional structure itself have been revealed in its implementation. National-state relations are ambiguous in many areas and will become more strained as the states become more effectively committed to the interests of their own linguistic regions. The President's Rule was originally an emergency provision when a breakdown in the constitutional procedures occurred. Its increasing use as an instrument of political manipulation in state politics may require further constitutional clarification.

More significant than the problem within the structure of the government however, is the fact that the government structure itself is a Western concept. It is different from traditional political processes more familiar to the Indian people. Thus it works more effectively as a structure when it functions on a national level, removed from the day to day political realities of India. The dynamics of the state legislative assemblies are more responsive to local and indigenous pressure groups, to factionalism, and village politics based on traditional, social relationships, than in the Lok Sabha, where the remoteness of national political life encourages more consistent and pro forma political activity. State politics are therefore much more fascinating to follow and are a better indicator of the process by which modern values and institutions are being adapted into the traditional patterns of political behavior.

A striking example of this disparity between constitutional consistency and political reality is in the role of the judiciary, India's Courts of Law. They are committed by the Constitution to defend basic individual human rights. But this concept is little understood by the mass of India's people. For them most legal claims or disputes are resolved by a council of elders of the caste-community, the *jati*, to which the people belong by birth. The elders enforce a strong sense of an individual's identity as an integral member of the community, not his rights as a separate and independent individual. The courts, then, by affirming the right of the individual before the law, separate themselves from this more immediate sense of social identity among the people. And, ironically, because the courts recognize individuals, not castes, they exclude the caste-communities from their jurisdiction. There is no constitutional, and hence no legal, provision to recognize and to limit the traditional prerogative of this caste group.

Because of this disparity between the formal constitutional structure of India as a democratic Republic and the actual, social-political life of the people, India is still a politically emerging nation. It still seeks its own political identity as a nation within the constitutional framework of a secular state. At the same time this framework is being drawn away from its western theoretical base to serve and express more adequately the distinct characteristics of the political styles in the caste and village.

A picture of India which portrays this two-way process of the traditional and modern interacting and changing each other is a useful way of describing what India is like. This image gives us some sense of the uneasy yet dynamic political reality which is India today.

We have looked at two different aspects of modern India: a picture of its economic development and problems; and a picture of its democratically elected, representative government. Economic and political development, however, do not present the total picture.

They are but two of several aspects of India we will explore. Each will complement the other. As the special character of each is added to the others, it will deepen our comprehension of the reality of India. An understanding of India can only be made on the basis of many such descriptions, one superimposed upon the other, until our comprehension becomes adequate to understand the fabric of Indian life.

QUESTIONS FOR DISCUSSION

1. Compare the political structure of India with that of the United States. What are the similarities and differences?

2. Do you feel that a two-party political organization is possible for India? Why or why not?

3. The author feels that state-federal relationships within India will be increasingly delicate in the years ahead. Can you suggest parallels here in United States history?

IV. THE VILLAGE

The economic and political structures which we discussed in the previous chapters select data that describe India as a people involved in the process of modernization. The traditional elements of India, most notably the social structure, provide the context into which modern ideas are introduced. In this context, new ideas are translated into uniquely Indian terms and are incorporated into Indian culture. To understand this traditional context of modernization, we will turn from the large scale of national politics and development to the village, the level on which these changes are actually taking place.

In proportion alone, the village is an essential fact of Indian life. Over three-fourths of the population live in 580,000 villages, which average less than one thousand people. This is in vivid contrast to our own situation, where over 70 percent of the United States' population live in urban areas. The migration trends in India are toward the cities, as indicated by the doubling of the populations in Calcutta, Delhi, and Madras during the past decade. As capital and industrial cities, they sustain a distinctive, cosmopolitan elite who are the forerunners of a modern Indian style. But most who move to the cities come in search of employment, leaving their families behind in the villages. And they retain a strong sense of their village identity. They seek out and dwell near members of their own village, forming extensions of the village patterns within the city. Those who find employment usually send back a portion of their earnings. And even whole families who have settled permanently in the city return to the village for important occasions, such as marriages or annual festivals. Thus even among the 20 percent of India's urban population, village identification is still immediate and vital.

To reach a village, we must first pass its cultivated lands, small patchwork plots outlined with mounds of packed dirt or small irrigation channels. Along these paths, we first encounter the life of the village. Its livelihood is drawn primarily from the soil, and much of the village activity occurs here. We see pairs of oxen pulling metal-tipped plows or people seeding with regular sweeps of the arms perhaps in cadence with a simple folk melody. Transplanting the rice seedlings and weeding are also done manually by rows of women dressed in saris of basic tone colors: orange, red, green, or blue. These women, bent at the waist, move in slow ranks across the water-soaked fields.

As the seeds begin to grow, painting the patches with vibrant shades of green, we can understand why village life in India is the source of so much romantic sentiment. The uncertainty of the rainfall and the anxious anticipation of the harvest only increase the villagers' closeness to the awesome forces of nature. A natural calamity becomes a human tragedy. The villager has found an almost heroic place among the urban elite and in the pages of India's modern literature. He is portrayed as a sincere and dedicated cultivator who, without question, sustains his marginal existence from the stingy soil. His unrewarded life, with its continuous taint of sorrow, expresses man's deep respect for his relentless struggle to survive.

Mango trees or coconut palms guide our way from the fields to the village itself. Small mud huts with roofs of palm boughs or corrugated tin make way occasionally for simple brick and stucco houses. Among these dwellings the romanticism of the paddy fields gives way to the jumbled, cheerful bounding of children. They stop and peer, their large brown eyes intent and "their faces holding curiosity like a cup." The persistent cawing of crows and the acrid smell of urine drying in the sun haunt our senses. We feel the continuous round of quiet, precise activity, made graceful through long practice. We see the potter lifting small clay pots from his wheel, the washerman wacking clothes against a rock at the side of a canal or village pond, and women swinging their water pots onto their heads at the well.

The normal round of ritual and chores reflects the rhythmic patterns of cultivation in the fields, patterns which are intensified at the time of harvest and major village festivals. But village life also reveals the infinite, spontaneous variations of human interaction which occur within an intricate pattern of social relationships.

For all people the most basic human relationships are in the family. Special feelings and expectations defined by various kinship roles are common to all of us. A man will quite naturally react differently to a woman, depending upon whether she is his wife, his younger sister, or his mother-in-law. In India, there are these same differences in responses, but the specific reactions in each role are quite different from ours. In the first place, child-rearing practices in India place far greater emphasis on the acceptance of parental authority and judgment. In the early years there are many subtle ways in which the superiority of the parent and the dependence of the child are reinforced. One of the most common is an almost univer-

Clemens Kalischer

Laundry in India hardly sees automatic washers and dryers. Here men clean their clothing by beating it against rocks.

sal unwillingness on the part of a parent to praise a child
or to encourage his initiative.

Another dramatic illustration of Indian and Western
differences is the practice of selecting husbands and wives.
We understand the choice of our prospective husband or
wife to be largely our own, and parental influence must
be both indirect and subtle to be effective at all. In India,
parents select a bride or groom for their children. Variations in this practice do occur. A liberal family may permit a child to meet his or her prospective spouse before
the wedding. The child may even exercise a veto if the parent's candidate does not meet with his approval. But the
basic pattern of parental responsibility for arranging a
marriage remains the common practice.

It seems very strange to us. But even Westernized students in India give valid reasons for the practice. In a society that allows few opportunities for boys and girls to
meet and talk freely outside of their own homes, these students are glad to have their parents conduct the search and
make the choice. Parents know their children well, have
their best interests at heart, and significantly, children
are prepared to respect their parent's judgment.

Another factor which favors the arranged marriage
over what Indians call "the love marriage," is the joint
family. Married children live with their parents. The joint
family works on two assumptions. The first is that a son
remains subservient to his father for his entire life, even
beyond the son's marriage. Marriage does not, as in our
society, place a son or daughter into an autonomous state
of adulthood. Secondly, the marriage relationship is sustained by the family as a whole, and not by an affection
bond between two individuals. A girl not only begins a
new life with the man she marries, but her life is caught
up in a whole series of relationships with others in the

family: with her mother-in-law, her husband's brothers, and their wives and children as well.

From our point of view, this concept of marriage is difficult to imagine. And indeed, if we tried to follow this practice without adopting other patterns and assumptions of Indian society, it would quickly prove intolerable for us. The reverse is also true. Without adopting our social presuppositions, particularly our ideas of individual independence and self-reliance, our marriage practices would prove equally unworkable in village India.

The limits of a joint family are hard to define. There always seems to be some distant cousin who arrives from some unexpected quarter, expecting to be received in the home. There are general limits to the family however. Generally, the members of a joint family are all of those who eat a meal cooked on a common fire. This definition recognizes the large number of rules and social expectations which govern dining in a traditional Indian home. But this definition also recognizes that the rules are applied with great flexibility, allowing the head of the household to determine in any given circumstance just how far he considers the limits of his family to extend.

Persons with whom marriage relationships are possible form another set of complex rules. These rules establish preferred mates recognizing that exceptions to practice are common. In south India, for example, the preferred mate for a son would be the daughter of his mother's brother. Other arrangements can, and frequently do, occur. Marriage to a daughter of his father's brothers, however, would be strictly forbidden.

In north India, a person also does not marry someone from his father's family. Nor does he marry someone from his own village. In both north and south he is expected to marry someone who belongs to his special group, known as a *jati* or caste community.

The jati is a family clan to which a person belongs by birth. The jati provides its members with a reservoir of preferred marriage mates. It also defines itself through a common occupation, such as farming, carpentry, cattle raising, or weaving. The jati, then, is an extended clan, one of several groups within the village. Since wives must come from outside the village, it also extends beyond the village. As a result, the jatis create webs of relationships that connect numerous neighboring villages.

The most distinctive characteristic of the jati is its function in the village, not its kinship base. In drawing together families which intermarry, the jati structure places its membership in a distinct social rank with respect to other jatis in the village. Everyone is thus placed by birth in a system which ranks the Brahmins, traditionally the priest community, at the top, other jatis in the middle, and the untouchables at the bottom. A person's interaction with anyone else in the village, who does not belong to his jati, will be influenced, if not actually determined, by their respective jati rank to each other. They cannot approach each other as equals except when they are small children.

The jati system thus provides those within the village with what we call horizontal linkages. Those who belong to a weaver's jati tend to live in the same part of the village, known as the weavers' quarter. The Brahmins also tend to reside in a special section closest to the village temple. And the untouchables are often found in a separate settlement some distance away.

Each jati has its own set of distinctive practices, its own dialect and dress, and its own leadership. A council of elders arbitrates disputes among its members and encourages those practices which maintain the distinctiveness and unity of the group. Irregularities or failure to observe its customs may be punished by the Council, even to the point of expulsion for a serious offender. Changes do occur, both in the rank of a particular jati with respect to other jatis, and in their eating habits, dress, and occupation. But these changes occur slowly and only with the concurrence of the group as a whole.

The criteria which rank one jati over another in a village are not clearly defined and vary greatly from one village to another. A particular jati of washermen, for example, in village A may find themselves ranked higher than the same jati with whom they exchange brides in village B. The Brahmins at the top and the socially unclean —the street sweepers, lavatory cleaners, and leather workers—at the bottom suggest a concern for ritual purity and freedom from pollution as the determining factors. But for the jatis in the middle—the cultivators, merchants, and village craftsmen—the relative purity of one over another may be based on a number of variable factors. A community of goatherders, for example, normally has a low rank in the village scale. Yet this jati successfully established a claim of high rank in the village of Kishan Garhi. Their claim is based on the acquisition of land, received through an auction some three generations ago. And in that same village, the carpenter jati shares equal status with the Brahmins in the eyes of some.

The ranking of these social groups with their self-enforcing unity enhances the stability of the village as a whole. Everyone has a place. But verticle movement, up and down, does occur. Since upward movement occurs at the expense of another jati, the tensions among jatis can be very great. Only with great reluctance, will one jati accept its own demotion. Without any clear or consistent standards of ranking, a constant dynamic among jatis occurs as one jati tests its status with other closely ranked jatis. This tension among the jatis explains why there is great resistance to the elevation of the untouchable communities to a more humane status in Indian society. The resistance comes not from those at the top, who by and large support the elimination of untouchability as a social evil. The resistance comes instead from those jatis who are immediately above the untouchables in the social scale. They see social uplift for the untouchables occurring at their own expense. Finding equal opportunity for minorities in the United States reveals a similar pattern. The greatest resistance comes from low-income groups who feel they would suffer economically by a change in the status of the minorities.

Perpendicular to the horizontally stratifying jati system are groupings which draw members of several jatis together. These vertical groups isolate members from others in their own jati. These groups are called *factions*. A person calls upon others to support him without regard to caste, usually in opposition to another member of his own jati. This appeal for intercaste support occurs most frequently today in an election campaign. But the practice has long been established in situations where two families are competing for control of their common jati, for a commonly claimed piece of land, or for redress of such grievances as failure to pay a debt or destruction of property.

The most extensive and binding of the factional alliances are based on the ownership of land. Landowners control the production and the distribution of grain, primary economic activities in any village. For many landholding families, this type of control is minimal since they own an average of one and a half acres. But those who have large holdings use a system of patronage called the *jajmani* system. These owners employ the services of others in the village in exchange for a fixed portion of the harvest.

The patronage system may also engage other villagers who perform services according to the traditional occupation of their jati. Thus, a carpenter, weaver, washerman, or sweeper may work for a portion of the harvest. Some may perform other services as well. The barber not only shaves his patron (jajman), but he is also expected, traditionally, to serve as the intermediary in negotiations which arrange for perspective brides for his patron's sons. Since no money is involved in any of the services, an employee tends to enter into a permanent relationship with a particular family or group of families. He will perform his service for them whenever it is needed and receive in return a continuous allotment of grain. Such relationships are often passed from one generation to another. The bonds established go far beyond the economic services involved. The relationships extend obligation and support in a wide variety of circumstances.

Large landholding families engage many members of different jatis in a village. Thus, the family's influence through the patronage system is extensive. Since members of the service jatis depend upon each other for their own needs, they are also involved in a network of interjati bonds. Thus the potential power of a landowner at the top can be great indeed.

A single jati of landowners and cultivators may be composed of several prominent families, and each will maintain an extensive group of villagers in its domain. The village, then, is not only horizontally divided into status-ranked jatis but is also divided into a series of vertical factions. And each faction has its own community of support drawn from several, if not all, levels of the jati hierarchy. The potential for power struggles is immense. Disputes over land are often the most intense and violent events in the life of a village. They become a source of severe and even open conflict between members of the same family.

The family, the jati, and the faction are the units of social structure in a typical Indian village. Village interaction occurs within these units, both the dramatic episodes and the hum of daily activities.

QUESTIONS FOR DISCUSSION

1. Imagine yourself in the place of an Indian student. You have just been told you are to be married at the end of the school year to someone selected for you. What emotions would you feel? What assumptions are involved in your reaction? Do you feel arranged marriages have merit over "love marriages?"

2. What are your reactions to the *jati* system? Does it have advantages? Do we have ways in the United States to classify people? Name some of these classes. How do you feel about these classifications?

V. MODERNIZATION IN THE VILLAGE

Modern technology has come to the village. New, high yielding strains of grain, fertilizer, and electrically powered water pumps have brought more food, employment, and hope. Schools have been built, and teachers have begun to number among the leading citizens of the village. Literacy and basic skills of farm and home management are taught to an increasing number of village children. And some of them will continue their studies in colleges for an active role in the developing urban and industrial life of their nation.

Crowded buses now rumble along an extensive network of rural highways, bringing inexpensive transport within reach of many villagers. They provide ready access to markets, urban employment, and new ideas. Bicycles, rare thirty years ago, are a common sight along the village lanes. They overtake a cheerful stream of laborers walking to the fields, or glide by a band of pilgrims in search of sacred places. They weave their way among the bullock carts piled high with straw, and dodge out of the path of the on-rushing buses, honking and scattering dust and startled chickens in their wake. Changes are taking place.

But these changes occur within patterns which have been established for generations and according to cultural norms which have evolved through centuries. Factional

politics as well as non-violent protest are both an integral
part of the life in modern India. This process of interaction and the resulting modification characterize the modern Indian scene. We also sense the resiliance and adaptability of the traditions of village life.

The most intense challenge of the modern era has
been the rapid increase in population. It has increased the
importance of the traditional factional groupings in the
village. As the population has increased, greater demands
have been placed upon the land; and more power has
come to those who control the distribution of its produce.
Faction leaders have thus acquired a stronger role, with
greater opportunity to enforce their dominance among
the villagers. The population challenge has forced existing social structures to respond. And insofar as these
structures proved adequate to the challenge, they have
found increased strength.

Other innovative forces of modern times have been
less intense and demanding. But in reaching the village,
they have been no less involved in its traditional patterns.
Where technological advances have made sense in terms
of these traditions, they have been widely adopted, and
their impact has been both helpful and constructive. But
where such innovations have come as a direct challenge to
accepted village norms, the results have not been so positive. Change, no matter how dramatic, has rarely happened outside the limits of accepted village norms.

One attempt to institute reform by direct confronta-
tion with traditional village practice has been a national
scheme to introduce cooperative farming. Adopted as a
policy of the government in its Community Development
Project, this plan encouraged the formation of common
ownership and cultivation of the lands of a village. And it
received funds in each of the first three Five Year Plans.

As a policy, cooperative farming appeared a much needed innovation. It would consolidate landholdings, usually small and fragmented, into more rational economic units. It would create the opportunity for better trained and more expert management, more efficient use of farm machinery, rotation of crops, and agricultural research. Its social implications also looked promising. Building upon a widely recognized sense of village identity, cooperative farms would increase the villagers' sense of participation in the life and welfare of the community as a whole. Sharing the lands and its produce could only stimulate a greater feeling of equality and mutual help. The project thus appeared as an effective means to overcome the factional and jati divisions within the village. It looked like a good instrument for social reform.

But the record of the cooperative farm program has not sustained its promise as a policy. In many instances, it was never tried because of rivalries between different arms of the government itself. Where it was implemented, actual results were far below the government's modest targets, achieving in some instances less than 25 percent of its goal. And as a national policy it has been all but abandoned.

There are a number of factors which have contributed to the program's failure. The economic goal of land consolidation was misdirected, aiming at greater efficiency, not the highest possible yield per acre. Yield per acre is not dependent upon the size of the plots used. Greater efficiency also means more use of labor saving machinery. But such is hardly a valuable goal in India. One of the greatest rural problems is the large number of unemployed laborers on the land already.

The cooperative farming project was also doomed in its goal to be an instrument of social reform. Its attempt to overcome the divisions and inequalities of the village factions and the jati social structure, even in the name of village solidarity, negated the very social groupings in which the traditional sense of village unity is normally expressed. Without the interaction provided by the factions and the jati hierarchy, there was no cohesive force within the village upon which a cooperative could be formed. The tradition of the village simply had no way of allowing a cooperative farm to happen.

As a result a more extensive government project for rural improvement has evolved. The government has specially trained Community Development workers to live and work with the villagers. These workers provide advice and encouragement to help the villagers overcome development problems on the local level. Their work has been quiet, and in some instances heroic. They have brought modern technology and government services in a way that would best serve the needs of each village.

But again, their impact has been limited. They have come from the outside as government workers into an already complex and cohesive social system. Their presence appeared both awkward and suspicious. Their greatest accomplishments have occurred where they have won the confidence of the village leaders. But in so doing, they have tended to give the advantage of their service and knowhow to those who could use it to strengthen their own position of dominance. Technological improvements, credit facilities, marketing advantages and others have been made available in the village. But the changes have come without any appreciable reform to the social structure. Modernization has thus tended to favor those who have the traditional authority and the skill to exercise village leadership. Those who gain the least are those already disadvantaged within the traditional social patterns of the village.

The extent of change on the village level is recorded in this recent report made by an American observer returning after eighteen years in a small North Indian village. The changes he records are substantial but done almost entirely within the structural patterns of the village.

> In 1962 an important event occurred. A farmer moved into the village who had never lived there before—a relative by marriage to some people who had lived there before. He was an ex-landlord from another part of the district and he bought about ten acres of land.

> He had tried some improved seeds and new fertilizer in 1961 in his own village. In 1962 he tried it in his new village and it was quite successful. The next year eight or ten other farmers tried it, and they too were successful. By 1964 everybody was falling over himself to get the new seeds and new fertilizers.

> This demonstration by one villager who had taken the initiative was extremely convincing.

> Their production has gone up—they saw they are getting at least twice what they were getting before—and they are certainly getting more than twice the money because prices have been rising all along. The price is about three times what it was.

> There are no empty fields these days. You see standing crops and people weeding and watering those crops. Labor is now being imported into the village. I met one farmer looking around the city trying to find somebody to bring back. He wanted to start a new tubewell and needed several laborers but could not find anybody in the village.

> The village has increased in population. It now

has about 40 percent more people than it had eighteen years ago. These are partly relatives, partly immigrants. More children have grown up but infant mortality is still extremely high and medical services have not improved.

The village headman is the one who came in and tried the new seed. He has completely, almost singlehandedly, abolished the factions in the village, because he has so much largesse to give out.

He was elected to the panchayat [village council] and when the village common lands were turned over to the panchayat there was a lot of land to sell. He gave them out to people who then became members of his faction. He sold them at low rates to the low castes and to the Muslims.

He put in quite a few paved streets and built a school. He has pleased people and they are eating out of his hand, but not in a dependent way—he has just got a good political base. The other faction really does not exist any more. There are a few discontented people, but they are doing quite well with their grinding mills and machinery. They simply do not have the land base that he has for power.

There is an awareness that there is something important in the village, an awareness of how customs differ from other peoples, an acceptance of urban standards as different from village standards, and a sense that the two ought to be related and are related. New things are coming in and there is local creativity.

A lot of this seems to have happened on its own power. The old society seems to have stepped up pretty much on the initiative of its own leadership, with a couple of new ideas here and there. It is a demonstration that it can work when people take over.

M. Marriott, "Is Village Life Changing?" (*Span.* July 1969).

One of the most significant instruments of change in this village and throughout India, has been the introduction of the ballot box. The Constitution of 1950, provided for every adult citizen the right to vote for candidates for public office. And the state Panchayat Acts during the 1950s, established an elected council of five members, called the *panchayat*, as the governing body in many villages. Democratic elections thus became the method of determining village leadership. And they were bound to have an impact on the style of village politics.

But even with such vital changes in political process, the existing village faction and jati structures still provide the most useful and natural groupings upon which to build popular support for public office. Thus existing social structures have provided an effective basis for the formation of voting blocks to assure the election of that candidate who, because of this support, would best represent their interests. These groupings have added to their traditional roles a function similar to that of ethnic and racial voting blocks within our own political parties. Without them, it is difficult to imagine how a democratically elected, representative government could ever have received wide acceptance among such a diverse, fragmented, and largely illiterate population.

Factional leaders have dominated the polls. They have simply converted their traditional claims of patronal allegiance to support for political office. And once elected, they use their office to protect their traditional prerogatives and interests. Strong faction leaders, for example, have been effective in weakening many of the laws which encourage more equitable land distribution. By virtue of their elected office they can oppose any limitation of their land holdings. Such limitations would reduce their economic strength and the base of their political power. Even when the new panchayat has worked to the benefit of the whole village, it has occurred because of an enlightened policy of a faction leader. The example of the village described earlier is a case in point. The new leader, by successfully introducing new ideas and methods, created a faction of his own.

Yet the democratic process is having its effect on faction leadership. It makes them more responsive to the needs and conflicting interests of their villages. Such responsiveness will increase as the power of the vote becomes better understood by those on the lower levels of the jati hierarchy.

The traditional jati structure is also responding to the new ways of selecting public officials. In many villages, jati members vote as a block when the jati is not divided by factions. And in villages where jatis of lower rank form a majority, their votes have, in some instances, elected a member to the panchayat.

Panchayats usually seek a consensus before taking action on an issue brought before them instead of deciding on the basis of a simple majority. Some panchayats with wide village representation have not been able to find a course of action upon which all members could agree. Such an impasse has limited the effectiveness of the council. But when agreement has been achieved, the interests of the poorer strata of the village have been served. In this way, the distribution of governmental services and the powers of local office have become wider. Yet the panchayat still favors those who succeed in getting their members elected to the council.

In elections above the village level, the jati system has greater impact. District, state, and national representatives require the support of more voters than even the most dominant village faction can muster. This need for wider support has given an added function to the jati web that stretches through several neighboring villages in search of wives for the village sons. These jati webs easily became the vehicle for the formation of political associations capable of uniting support for a single candidate over a wider region. Members of a jati sought out their caste counterparts in other villages to protect their interests in state and national legislatures. Caste associations have thus become a fact of Indian politics today, even serving as lobbying groups when they have not been able to elect their own members to public office.

Because these associations are geographically spread out and political in purpose, their bonds are looser than the kinship ties on which they have been built. But since they do incorporate traditional relationships, they have greater unity and stability than alliances formed only for political purposes. The jati system has thus provided an effective base so that the orderly conduct of democratic elections and representative government can function. And villagers have been involved by building on their participation in jati interaction. What is familiar has become an effective means to introduce a new form of political activity.

As we might expect, the jati system influences the types of issues that can become the appropriate concern of the government. Their effective handling of disputes among their members, as we have seen, has lessened the impact of an individual's legal rights provided by the Constitution. The system has also prevented legislative action on some of the most difficult village problems: unemployment, the inequities of wealth and privileges, and landowner-laborer relations. These issues have been left largely unresolved. Disputes between landowners and laborers, for example, are still mostly resolved by force.

Village politics, factional alliances, and the jati structure effectively function on the national level as well. The interaction between traditional politics and the new structures of the Constitution is an important drama in India. The situation will become more intense as new political figures rise to national prominence and participate in the decisions of national government. Most of the legislators of the early post-independence years were schooled in Western political philosophy and British parliamentary procedure. The new leaders have developed their prowess in the political arena of the village and state. The old leaders based their success on their standing for the most advantageous or productive issues in a campaign. The success of the new leaders is their ability to function within the traditional social groups as they adapt to new political realities.

Hope that an accommodation can be reached between the new politics and the traditional is based in part on the nature of the democratic process itself. This process makes the activity of government answerable to the local arena. And the adaptability of the village traditions also suggests that local politics will continue to adjust to democratization. This movement on both sides can be seen throughout India. Effective exercise of leadership within traditional patterns is a significant and widespread evolution. And the overall picture supports the impression of orderly and consistent development.

But it is not the whole story. In other places, the landless and other poor have yet to receive the benefits of political power. They express an uneasiness and dissatisfaction with the present process of change. Some have been able to demand collectively a greater share of the increased produce. But where they have been most effective, friction with the landholding jatis has developed; and the orderly processes of society have given way to violence.

These tensions will increase as such groups become larger and better organized and as their expectations for fulfillment rise.

An indication of this growing uneasiness is recorded in a simple village song, translated by an American student working in a school committed to the non-violent teachings of Gandhi. The American writes:

> At the school there is much singing particularly in the evening before we all go to sleep and the jackals in the forest begin their night laughter. To sing here is important. Children learn folksongs before they learn to count. As my Hindi gets better, I've begun to translate some of these. There is one that had particular interest for me because despite all their talk of non-violence it shows the reverse anger which is still in many of these people. It is called "In the Other Side" and they teach it to their kids. It goes:

> O God, what is in your blind world!
> In one side . . .
> > I saw ruined huts.
> And in the other wide . . .
> > Silken curtains hanging on one man's door.
> In the one side . . .
> > I saw broken beams and earthen walls.
> In the other side . . .
> > O God there were high buildings with electric bulbs burning all around.
> In one side . . .
> > More ruined and damaged huts.
> In the other side . . .
> > There were buildings like castles with all people in beautiful and charming dress.

> In one side . . .
>> A naked boy and girl.
> O God, what is in the other side?[5]

The orderly growth and stability of India today is due in many ways to the depth and strength of its traditions. At the same time we can sense that India's historic patterns and norms have yet to resolve the challenges presented by the modern era.

QUESTIONS FOR DISCUSSION

1. The social disruption and upheaval which accompanies the introduction of modernization in any country, but particularly in Third World countries, raises questions about whether modernization should be imposed on others. This concern is expressed in many ways: Are developing countries ready for democracy? Should the United States defend another country's right to self-determination? If so, how should other countries determine their own public will?

2. Is technological change or advancement an improvement for traditional societies? Can they adapt and retain their traditional character?

3. Should the United States impose its values on another country? Should we prevent another country from modernizing? Or modernizing on its own terms?

VI. RELIGION IN THE VILLAGE *8*

In the early spring of 1970, the governing council of Madurai, a city in southern India, found itself faced with a difficult political problem. The area had received little rain during the monsoon seasons of 1968 and 1969, and the city was in the midst of a severe drought.

The problem facing the council was critical. Popular and classical traditions have long stated that the quality of leadership can be evaluated through natural conditions. Through the righteousness of a good king's rule, he sees to the welfare of his subjects and enlists the cooperation of the natural elements on their behalf. It was, therefore, quite in keeping with tradition for the people to look to their government for relief from the drought. During the spring of 1970, popular sentiment had determined the specific cause of the drought and the people were agitating for action.

In a city square, some four blocks from the temple, was a large stone statue of an elephant. Several years earlier, the statue had been turned around, apparently for aesthetic reasons, so that the elephant's triumphant trunk instead of its cumbersome rear faced the square. The people felt that the goddess enshrined in the temple had been displeased by this change and was withholding the rains from the city.

The council, on the one hand, did not want to encourage the expression of popular religious beliefs as a significant factor in the administration of government. It was committed to secular rule, capable of serving all elements of the society, instead of catering to the sentiments of any particular religious group. On the other hand, the elephant-has-caused-the-drought feeling represented a growing conviction of the people the council had been elected to serve.

The solution was to arrange for street workers to work through the night, reversing the position of the elephant. The feelings of the people were respected, but in a way that caused as little public notice as possible. This procedure alleviated possible friction among religious groups and disassociated the council from the act. One March morning, people entering the square found the elephant facing away from the square. And that very day and for the following week, it rained in the city of Madurai.

A visitor to an Indian community is impressed by the many diverse religious objects that surround him. His path is lined with shrines of various shapes and sizes: a polished stone decorated with a faded, dry garland, a tree surrounded by a red-powdered wrought iron fence of snakes, or an ornately carved temple gateway, projecting high into a cloudless blue sky. All of these objects proclaim a powerful but mysterious presence which is recognized and honored by the villagers in acts of respect, prayer, and worship.

Households abound with ceremonies. Some are ornate, like a wedding, or the annual family rite in memory of a deceased father. Some are very simple. A landless laborer makes a plea for work before a crudely formed, mud image of the elephant-headed god, *Ganapati*, the remover of obstacles. The preparation of a meal, the devotion of a wife, and the patient attentiveness of a daughter-in-law may all be acts of worship, expressed in the daily round of activities that sustain God's blessing. The grateful visitor may feel rebuffed by his village host's response to an expression of thanks when the host replies, "It is my duty." He means that he did not receive the visitor in order to gain his favor or make the visitor beholden to him. The host accepts his guest as a religious act in the sincere faith that every guest brings to his home an intimation of the divine.

Much of the religious activity in the village is in response to the recurring crises which visit all homes at random but with inevitable certainty: accidents, losses, disease, hostility, hunger, and death. Being a simple people, these crises are understood as the work of unknown, evil spirits, or an uncompromising fate—all hidden powers which lurk in the dark corners of the world, ready to work some mischief or harm.

The people, therefore, feel it is necessary to propitiate or avert the anger of these forces. The most important figure on this level of religious concern is the *shaman*. He is a man periodically possessed by a hidden spirit, through whom the evil spirit can be identified and the appropriate means disclosed by which it can be placated.

The shaman does not normally acquire a religious role by birth or profession. Rather, he discovers through a unique experience, a trance, or a vision, that he is endowed with powers to cope, if not with the calamity itself, at least with the emotional needs of those who experience it. He may at first serve as an apprentice with an established shaman and later gather a clientele whom he serves whenever called upon. But his religious authority depends upon his ability to identify the source of evil and respond with an appropriate remedy. Insofar as the shaman succeeds, he remains an effective emissary of sacred power and has the ability to avert or control evil in the lives of the village people.

More formal religious expressions are made to specific deities to avert misfortune. Small shrines have been built in which special ceremonies are performed at consistent intervals to these deities to ward off their evil powers. Propitiatory rites, for example, are offered to the goddess of smallpox in some villages at a set time of the year. These rites are an integral part of the village festival calendar.

The traditional character and regularity of these festivals lead us to another level of religious awareness. The villagers gain a sense of an ordered and benevolent rhythm of nature through these annual village festivals. The purpose of these rites is to enter into an established pattern already divinely ordained and sustained by the activity of the gods. The celebration of these rites is thus identified with some mythological account of a specific act of the gods on behalf of man. And the ceremonies occur at a specific time during the year to reenact that act of grace on the part of past heroes or the gods. A villager does not change the course of the gods' activity but participates with them so that he may share in the bounty of their beneficent power. The whole cycle of ceremonies associated with planting and the harvest are examples of this type of religious activity.

Each festival has distinctive aspects: a specific set and sequence of ceremonies, special foods, or specific members of the family or community who participate. A ceremony may be very simple. In one, only the mother of the family fasts all day and goes outside after dark to look at the moon through a sieve before rejoining her family at dinner.

Other festivals are national like our Thanksgiving or even like our summer holidays, celebrated in distinctive ways in different parts of the country. But everyone participates in some way or another. *Deepavali*, or the Festival of Lights, is celebrated in November by decorating houses with row upon row of tiny lamps, sparkling in the soft, crisp evening air. In the towns and cities, firecrackers burst through the night, proclaiming a sense of joy and excitement. And during the day, members of the family exchange gifts of new clothes.

An even more colorful celebration is the Festival of Holi, a spring rite celebrated widely throughout northern India. Children run through the streets spraying red dye on anyone within range. The village becomes a topsy turvy world where wives beat their husbands and all ages dance and sing in the streets.

Another widely celebrated festival is called, *Dasahra*, or *Navaratri*. It reenacts a tremendous mythological battle and final victory of Rama. Rama is the divine hero of India's great epic, the *Ramayana*. In this myth, Rama conquers Ravana, a demonic king who abducted Rama's wife, Sita. During late September or early October, large papier-maché figures of these two protagonists and accompanying heroes are made in Delhi, and the battle enacted on the great *maidan* (parade ground) before the Red Fort. The festival ends with the figure of Ravana and his cohorts being blown to pieces by explosives planted inside the papier-maché figures.

The spirit of the attending crowds is more festive and gay than we would expect in a religious ceremony. There is little reverence. But it is as significant as any other ceremony which celebrates the victory of good in the universe over the forces of evil. Rama's victory is assured, and so the people enjoy it. They are assured in their faith that whatever may occur to them in the future, the ultimate victory is with Rama and the forces of good which are arrayed on his side.

The celebration of the triumph of good over evil, as the central theme, can be seen in many other festivals held at different times of the year in various villages of India. This type of festival occurs especially during the fall months, when the southward course of the sun draws it closer to the southern horizon. The people celebrate the efforts of divine beings to bring it back to the peak of the sky.

Another type of festival which occurs in temples throughout southern India during the fallow spring months is the celebration of the divine marriage of a principal god or goddess and his or her consort. Again, it is a religious act in which the people participate, where the primary action is recorded in a mythological account, and is now reenacted for the purpose of allowing the people to enter into its sacredness and share in its beneficence. The rite serves as a divine prototype for the marriages of the people. Marriage is made more sacred by the example of the gods.

There is a third level of religious expression in the village, distinct from the crisis-oriented practice of the shaman and the more traditional patterns and corporate activity of the festivals. This third type is structured in elaborate sacrificial rituals over which the traditional priesthood, the Brahmins, preside.

These rituals are evident in the temple festivals of the village. These festivals usually last for several days and involve a special traditional role for almost every member of the village: as musicians, temple cart pullers, or as patrons of particular parts of the ceremonies. But the central focus of this village celebration is an elaborate series of religious acts performed by the priesthood. These rituals are intricate acts of pouring or placing symbolic elements into a sacred fire, elements such as water, specially prepared butter (called ghee), grains, seeds, rice, all in a highly ritualized sequence. These acts are performed according to manuals of ritual which are centuries old and are accompanied by the precise recitation of India's most ancient and sacred literature, hymns of the *Rig Veda*.

The reverence and sense of awe which these rituals stir among the people is immense. During the final hours of such a ceremony, tremors of excitement, apprehension, and exhileration move through the crowds, as they press in on all sides waiting for the most sacred moments of the ceremony. Sacred power is here not being placated, nor celebrated, but is being created before the eyes of the devout beholders. And its presence calls forth from the villagers a profound feeling of wonder and of worship.

Part of the sacredness of this ritual is identified with the priest. Its effectiveness depends upon both his long instruction in the intricacy of the performance and his sacred purity. He maintains his purity by adhering to a distinct and rigid set of religious and social practices which characterize Brahmin orthodoxy. The priest maintains a vegetarian diet and performs a number of cleansing rituals in his daily, household rites. He may also practice austerities and meditation to enhance his religious understanding and purity. By these acts his authority is recognized, and they assure the high ranking of the Brahmin community in the social hierarchy of the village.

More importantly is the symbolic content of the sacrifice itself. For the sacred power generated in the performance of the sacrifice called the *Brahman* is equated in the ancient religious tradition of India with the transcendent power which created the entire universe. *Brah-*

man of the sacrifice is the One, the Ultimate Reality, the source of all being.

The effective expression of religious power in the Brahmanic sacrifice, continually affirms a sacredness that cannot be contained in ordinary, daily experience, even when it is directed toward a desirable economic or political goal. This ritual act rather points beyond itself to a level of experience which relates man to a transcending sense of reality. It extends his fingertips even to the edges of the universe.

> The same stream of life that runs through my veins night and day runs through the world and dances in rhythmic measures.
>
> It is the same life that shoots in joy through the dust on the earth in numberless blades of grass and breaks into tumultuous waves of leaves and flowers.
>
> It is the same life that is rocked in the ocean cradle of birth and death, in ebb and in flow.
>
> I feel my limbs are made glorious by the touch of this world of life. And my pride is from the life-throb of ages dancing in my blood this moment.
>
> Rabindranath Tagore "Gitanjali," LXIX.

QUESTIONS FOR DISCUSSION

1. What is your reaction to the role of the shaman? Are there individuals in United States' society who perform a similar function? If so, what is your reaction to them? Explain.

2. What do you consider sacred? What activities or ideas are used to represent its sacredness? According to an ancient Indian religious tradition, all of life is a sacrifice. What does this mean to you?

3. New Year celebrations are among the most ancient religious festivals known to man, particularly agricultural man. What do they symbolize? What do New Year festivals in this country symbolize?

VII. THE CLASSICAL TRADITION
IN INDIAN SOCIETY

The preeminent social position of the Brahmin priesthood has its origin deep in India's traditional past. Their distinctive role goes back to the rustic courts of the tribal princes during the early Aryan period (1500-500 B.C.). Royal priests had the vital function of establishing religious authority for their leaders. If these princes were endowed with sacred power, they would rule successfully over both their subjects and their rivals.

To fulfill this function, the priests gathered many popular and courtly religious practices into a complex series of rituals to consecrate their leader, to promote his rule, and to celebrate his achievements. Ceremonies of coronation with sacred water, of welfare with an intoxicating plant called soma, and of victory with the sacrifice of a stallion—all served to express the sacred power with which the king ruled. And the priests traced the king's power to the deities or the religious powers with whom they as priests were identified. Thus, very early in the course of India's history, the priests assumed an important place in the maintenance of social order and welfare.

Their position was further enhanced in the deepening awareness of the relationship between the authority of their king and the power of creation. The connection between these two forces, royal authority and creation, was the Brahman, the holy power of the sacrifice itself.

This identification in the royal sacrifice of the original act of creation is celebrated in a series of later hymns in the *Rig Veda.* The collection includes many hymns and fragments probably compiled in the form in which we now have it around 1000 B.C., but many hymns are much older. Hymn 90 in the Tenth Book, describes the entire universe as having been initially embodied within an ideal, universal, archetypal figure of man called *Purusha:*

> The Purusha alone is all this universe, what has been, and what is to be. . . . A quarter of him is all beings, three quarters are the immortal in heaven.

The sacrifice of this heavenly archetypal figure of man then led to the creation of the world. Different objects in the universe were the symbolic representations of specific parts of his sacrificial body:

> The moon sprang from his mind, the sun was produced from his eye.

Significantly, the earliest statement of the traditional *varna* scale is found in this poem. This scale ranks society into four hereditary groupings in order of precedence as Brahmins (priests), Kshatriyas (rulers), Vaisyas (citizens), and Sudras (laborers). In this ancient account, the Brahmins are portrayed as his spokesman, his mouth. The rulers are his arms; the citizens, merchants, and landowners, his legs; the laborers are portrayed as his feet.

The hierarchical character of this ranking, a fundamental assumption of Indian society, is quite distinct from our own assumption that all men are created equal. It asserts that the structure of an ordered society ought to be built upon the premise that among men there is a wide discrepancy in both potential and opportunity. Man lives in greater harmony and has greater opportunity to fulfill himself when he accepts the circumstances, both social and natural, into which he has been born.

Our belief in the equality of all men is based, as in the Declaration of Independence, upon a religious-cultural premise. In India, the social ranking of the caste system is based on the sacred authority of this hymn. The origin of the position of the Brahmin community is in the very order of things in the world.

Because of this religious basis, it is important to distinguish between this ancient *varna* scale and the jati social structure. In terms of numbers alone, there is a vast difference. Rather than dividing society into four distinct hereditary groups, the jati system attempts to describe the social interaction among a large number of extended kinship groups. Such interaction may involve approximately twenty jatis in any one village and over three thousand jatis throughout India. The two systems involve different concepts of what the essential social groupings are.

The *varna* scale has been superimposed upon the jati structure in important ways and illustrates how the norms of the classical tradition vitally enter into village life. For example, the *varna* scale identifies the sacrificial role of the Brahmin priests as a significant factor which sustains these communities at the top of the jati structure. Beneath them, the varna scale and the jati system do not correspond so clearly. For the jatis exhibit greater flux among themselves than the fourfold structure of the *varna* scale would indicate. Studies of jati structure in the village do indicate a general fourfold division. But in terms of the *varna* scale, these divisions identify jatis grouped together in this way: highest, Brahmin jatis; high or clean laborer jatis; low or unclean laborer jatis; and lowest, untouchable jatis.

There are, however, a number of non-Brahmin jati communities which, because they have achieved a position of dominance in their village, advance a claim to royal *varna* background. It is difficult for them to substantiate this claim either by tradition or heredity. The claim is based instead on the alignment of their present status according to the *varna* scale. The mobility of any jati involves just this process. It claims a position of higher correspondence on the *varna* scale than it now has. There are instances where jati communities have even achieved Brahmin rank by carefully imitating the social practices of the traditional Brahmin communities.

There is good evidence to suggest that this practice has generally been the case. None of the great imperial dynasties of India, for example, were of royal background. The Mauryans appear to have been from a community assigned to the laborer level of caste, and the Guptas were from the merchant level. Their royal position thus appears to have been a status to which they rose through their acquisition of imperial rule.

The lack of direct correspondence between the *varna* scale and the actual social interaction, however, has not diminished the importance of this scale in the tradition. It was not conceived to be an accurate description of what the world is actually like. Its authority rather rested in its ability to express insight into the sacred reality from which all creation springs.

In the classical period of India, this sacred fourfold order was thus not only sustained but greatly elaborated in a series of treatises called *Dharmasastras*, or law books. These texts developed an elaborate system of appropriate behavior for each of the four castes in such a way that the hierarchical ranking among them was both visible and assured.

The greatest of these texts is called the *Law of Manu,* and dates from around the third century A.D. It begins with a description of creation, affirming the religious basis of the fourfold rank. And it maintains this explicit gradation by setting forth specific rules of conduct for the vital stages in the life of the top three castes. This distinction is most dramatically obvious in terms of punishments for the same offence. When a Brahmin commits an offense against a laborer, for example, he receives a reprimand, whereas a laborer may receive death if he offends a Brahmin.

The Laws of Manu differentiates between stages in a man's life and distinguishes between the appropriate behavior expected for each of them. These stages, called *ashramas,* are: studentship, householder, mendicant, and ascetic. Each stage lasts twenty-five years in a full life of one hundred. There are distinctive characteristics in each of the stages. Celibacy is to be maintained during the first and last two stages, but not during the second. A man is expected to be a provider only during the householder stage. Thus a person acts according to two sets of rules: his rank, determined by birth; and his life stage.

There are other variables built into this system, even a special set of rules to cover times of adversity and distress. All add to the complexity of the system. But they also make it more comprehensive and workable by avoiding the rigidity of a system of social mores that assumes a common rule for all people, whatever their age and walk of life.

This comprehensive structure is an impressive intellectual accomplishment. It reveals care and discernment by observation of what happens in the everyday world. But it also reveals that these classical scholar-priests did not find, in natural social behavior, a basis for consistency and order. Natural human behavior never became a detached, objective model to be followed. Because they had a strong sense of the flux and uncertainty of our experience, order was sought elsewhere, in more abstract, intellectual analyses. It was through such analysis that Indian culture contributed the concept of the number 0 to our mathematical system. The Roman system, for instance, had no such concept.

These analyses did not have their authority in their correspondence with nature. It was rather in the depth of insight as an abstract, intellectual norm, based on different aspects of human experience which won admiration and positions of respect in the tradition.

The *Laws of Manu* is but one of several examples in the classical tradition of such analysis. The *Arthasastra* is a treatise on the art of statecraft. It builds its analysis on the assumption that a king has no other source of power than the exercise of his own authority. It sets forward an extensive set of rules for the orderly maintenance of a kingdom in what must be considered one of man's great literary monuments to political pragmatism.

Poetics is another area which is defined with extensive precision in the classical period. Literary works are classified according to the dominant emotion which the poet communicates to his audience. And the merit of his work is determined by the skill exhibited in combining image and sound in the refinement of that emotion into an exquisite expression of beauty. And the list could go on to art, music, and philosophy.

Of all the accomplishments of abstract elaboration in the classical tradition, none is greater than the earliest, the perceptive analysis and structure of language by the classical grammarians. Their skill almost literally created their classical language called Sanskrit.

The word *sanskrita* means made together, formed, or perfected. As a language, it is formed according
to precise, elaborate, and consistent patterns of linguistic
behavior. The analyses of these patterns evolved over a
long period of time and reflect the great and early concern
on the part of the traditional priesthood to preserve the
precise recitation of the Rig Veda hymns used in the sacrifice. These analyses were collected into a single formula-
tion by the grammarian Panini, who probably lived during the fourth century B.C. His analysis of language led
to an ingenious and highly effective, description of how
language functions.

Panini's concern was to analyze how sounds, as the
basic structural units of language, fit together to form a
word or a sentence. For only specific combinations of
sounds form words, and specific combinations of words,
sentences. Words and sentences thus have their own patterns of use and consistency. These patterns are related to
what and how we experience things, but they are determined by the character of language itself. He was not
concerned about how particular words express this or
that meaning which is, to some degree, arbitrary and yet
constantly changing. The permanent structures in language were what he sought to explain.

The result of Panini's analysis of language was a
profound understanding of its structural nature which he
codified into a set of rules for the use of Sanskrit. So complete was this analysis, that he halted any further evolution in its form. All of the patterns of its structure had been
discovered, and it had thus reached its perfection as a linguistic system. Such an accomplishment ranks Panini
among the greatest of the world's ancient scholars, one
whose insights, as in the case of Plato, are still being discovered and appreciated.

The explorations of scholar-priests into the abstract structures of human experience which produced these social, political, aesthetic, and linguistic treatises are a vital part of India's heritage. And they represent only a few of the many classical works, which include outstanding literary, artistic, and philosophical masterpieces as well. Space does not permit any introduction to the Sanskrit poems of Kalidasa, the philosophy of Sankara, or the majestic tranquility portrayed in the sculpture of the seated Buddha of Sarnath. All of these works belong among the finest endeavors which the human imagination has produced. And the people of India are justly proud of them.

A more subtle impact of this tradition on contemporary India is the concept of *symbol*. The classical scholars assumed that man's greatest insights into the nature of reality are expressed in symbols rather than as facts. They did not attempt to objectify everything in their experience and to see what made it work. They sought to discover in their experience a deeper level of meaning, a meaning which pointed beyond itself to its truth.

This quest for the true meaning of experience in the world has been pursued in many ways throughout India's long history: from the abstract analysis of social behavior to explorations into the depths of human consciousness. A clear example of its introduction into the modern world is in the quest of the leader of India's independence movement, (Mahatma) Mohandas K. Gandhi.

Gandhi's understanding of the classical tradition was in many ways more intuitive than informed. He had never been trained in its intricacies. But there were a number of instances in which he identified not only the specific content of the tradition but also a sense of its symbolic character. Becoming a free nation was, for example, more significant to him as a symbol of true freedom among the people than as a political fact.

This symbolic sense of becoming a nation so influenced his political thought that he performed a whole series of acts which were designed to point beyond political autonomy to a sense of self-respect, moral responsibility, and social harmony. For example, he promoted the spinning wheel as a symbol of India's national life. It encouraged local production of cotton thread as an alternative to buying cloth from British mills. It was an act of political defiance that protested the economic control the British exercised over Indian life. But spinning is also a simple act that all can do and one from which they can see positive results. It is productive and vital to human welfare and it encourages self-sufficiency. Spinning thus encouraged virtues which were as essential to India's independence as was freedom from British domination.

The protest Salt March of 1931, is another example of Gandhi's non-violent tactics. He led a procession of thousands to extract salt from the sea. This salt thus produced could not be taxed. It was an act to assert India's freedom from British rule. Like his other protest campaigns, the march revealed the strong, peaceful character of the Indian people, demonstrating their capacity for independence in a symbolic way. Gandhi called these non-violent campaigns *satyagraha*, or acts of truth.

An equally vital part of Gandhi's concept of freedom was the need for reform in India's society. For him, reform was a necessary step before a meaningful independence. In particular, he was disturbed by the repression of the untouchable communities. He called it, "the ulcer of untouchability."

His concern for the plight of the untouchables was demonstrated in many ways. He welcomed them into his

Mahatma Gandhi is shown here at his spinning, a duty which he continued in his campaign for the production of home goods.

religious community, calling them Harijans, or children of God. He would not permit any form of discrimination by other members. And he led non-violent campaigns so that the untouchables could enter Hindu temples.

Significantly, he never advocated the elimination of the *varna* caste structure. What needed to be removed was the inequality in the jati system. Gandhi felt that the classical caste divisions were necessary to preserve a sense of social interdependence and mutual concern essential to the working of a true democracy. But the feelings of superiority had to be rooted out to allow the varna caste model to express the classical ideal of social harmony.

> I believe that caste has saved Hinduism from disintegration. But like every other institution it has suffered from excrescences. I consider the four divisions alone to be fundamental, natural and essential. The innumerable subcastes are sometimes a convenience, often a hindrance. The sooner there is fusion the better. The silent destruction and reconstruction of subcastes have ever gone on and are bound to continue. Social pressure and public opinion can be trusted to deal with the problem. But I am certainly against any attempt at destroying the fundamental divisions. The caste system is not based on inequality, there is no question of inferiority, and so far as there is any such question arising, the tendency should undoubtedly be checked. But there appears to be no valid reason for ending the system because of its abuse. It lends itself easily to reformation. The spirit of democracy, which is fast spreading throughout India, and the rest of the world, will, without a shadow of doubt, purge the institution of the idea of predominance and subordination.

The spirit of democracy is not a mechanical thing
to be adjusted by abolition of forms. It requires
change of the heart.

Mason, ed., *India and Ceylon: Unity and Diversity* (Oxford:
Oxford University Press. 1967).

QUESTIONS FOR DISCUSSION

1. We can all recognize India's outstanding achievements in
   analytical thought and symbolic understanding. But how
   do you account for India's lack of development in natural
   science? What can we say about Western culture that explains this difference in intellectual development?

2. Gandhi is an admired figure throughout the world. Yet his
   non-violent methods as political tactics are still controver-
   sial. Can you name people or social movements that have
   used his methods? Have they been successful? Why? Do you
   think Gandhi's methods would still be effective for oppress-
   ed groups within a nation? For a nation? Why?

VIII. MODERN INDIA

In the course of this study, we have looked at a wide view of modern India. It has ranged from an economic picture to Gandhi's non-violent expression of India's nationalism. We have covered a wide spectrum of detail and concept to express both the diversity and interrelatedness of many aspects of Indian life. But even in their complexity, the aspects we have chosen barely touch upon the living reality of India to the perceptive visitor. For such a visitor, Indian life reflects the infinite and intricate variety which characterizes all human life. The totality of India is no less elusive than life itself.

We can see this elusive character of India through a brief look at the India-Pakistan situation in their common quest for political stability. The hope for stability in the subcontinent through political unification caused many in India to lament the partition of the area in 1947, into two separate nations, India and Pakistan. The division seemed a violation of its cultural integrity as a civilization.

The vast displacement of people involved the migration and repatriation of nearly ten million people and the violent and senseless deaths of many hundreds of thousands. Such human misery only aggravated the sense of disjunction, leaving a scar of partition far deeper than the balm of independence could soothe. Bangladesh has now come into being as a third nation after nine months of in-

credible bloodshed. To those who sense India's whole-
ness, this continued political division is an agonizing
reality among a people who would seem to be one.

And yet at few times in the history of the subcontinent have even large portions been under the control of a
single political authority. The Emperor Asoka (247-237
B.C.), the last member of the Mauryan Dynasty came the
closest. He extended his rule throughout all but the
southern half of the peninsula. Rock and pillar edicts
bear his name and instructions in many corners of the
land. His rule is distinctive because, in the middle of his
reign, Asoka abandoned military force as a means of extending his rule. He preferred to lead subjects by good will
and the Holy Law of Buddhism. His renunciation of the
use of force in the name of public order and religious truth
makes Asoka one of the rarest of the world's great leaders.
He was revered as much in his own time as he is in India
today. Yet, his empire barely survived his death.

It was not until the time of the Gupta dynasty, in the
fourth and fifth centuries A.D., that an imperial kingdom
again approached the size of the Mauryan Empire. This
period brought great artistic achievement in sculpture
and in the literary works of India's great Sanskrit poet,
Kalidasa. Its political significance, however, was limited;
and the subcontinent was soon divided into many smaller
kingdoms.

And so it remained until the reign of Akbar, (1556-
1603) second of the Moghul kings, who established the
longest political succession in India, extending into the
nineteenth century. Akbar was, like Asoka, noted for his
tolerance and universalist understanding of religion. He
also utilized highly effective systems of district administration and political consolidation. The splendor and dy-
namism of his court were a marvel to visitors from around

the world. And he encouraged an artistic tradition. The elegantly beautiful Taj Mahal, the masterpiece built by his grandson, Shah Jahan, is the most fitting and eloquent monument.

The rule of the Moghuls in southern India was limited, however. The political consolidation of this region was accomplished only by the British Indian Empire from 1857 to 1947. It was built upon the increasing administrative involvement of the East India Company in the late eighteenth century. Even though its presence was felt throughout the subcontinent, the British Raj system, at its height, had only three-fifths of the subcontinent under control. The rest remained under the control of an array of hereditary Maharajahs.

The founders of Pakistan saw themselves in 1947, as heirs to the autonomous Islamic rule of the Moghul Empire. A separate state seemed a wiser course to insure the stability of the subcontinent in view of the potential unrest of a large Muslim minority subjected to the majority rule of a Hindu population.

The boundaries between India and Pakistan were drawn by grouping the adjacent districts of British rule where the Muslims were in clear majority. This criterion created an eastern and western wing of an Islamic nation (Pakistan) separated by more than one thousand miles of Indian soil. The 1947 partition thus divided the subcontinent in two. The independence of Bangladesh in 1971, reveals the difficulty of dividing into two what is in fact many.

The picture of India becomes even more complex when the linguistic areas are introduced. It is possible to distinguish between two major linguistic families: Indo-European in the north and the Dravidian in the south. About 75 percent of the population speak Indo-European languages, and approximately 23 percent speak one of the four Dravidian languages. The language division lines do not correspond with those of religion or geography. Therefore, language presents another basis for division in the subcontinent.

India, then, sustains many diverse images of its identity, and we have explored only a few. What unity is expressed occurs through the interaction of at least the three distinct images we have discussed in our study, images of the modern, village, and classical aspects of its culture.

In several areas of this study, we have mentioned Mahatma Gandhi. For us, he embodies the complexity and vitality of India better than any other image or description. Gandhi understood the people's aspirations and the requirements for a modern, politically viable nation. At the same time, he understood and could express these goals in terms which the people could appropriate. Gandhi's genius is that he fused together India's historic traditions and institutions with her modern aspirations. In his political organization during the 1920s, for example, he bypassed the administrative divisions of the hereditary kingdoms and British provinces. He based his political organization on the linguistic areas of the subcontinent. Gandhi thereby gave the original impetus to linguistic regionalism, one of the most explosive and divisive elements in national Indian life today. Yet, this organization mobilized the people and gave the independence movement a following it could not have obtained on any other basis.

Through Gandhi's leadership, independence and freedom became a quest for a more profound and sacred India. This emerging India would be realized in social harmony, built upon respect for the other person. Such respect was the basic premise for Gandhi's non-violent action.

It was in this vision of India's future that on the day

of independence, Gandhi was not to be found in the capital, but in a village of Bengal. He was pleading with the people there not to be caught up in the rash wave of violence which swept across the northern plains in the wake of the India-Pakistan partition.

Mahatma Gandhi stands today as a symbol of what India can become as a nation with an identity of its own among the nations. Throughout history, India has experienced an immense diversity. There is little known in the world that has not crossed its borders, from the accumulated lore brought by the ancient bunder boats that plied their slow but persistent course from Africa to the Indonesian isles, to marauding Turks seeking refuge from the rugged steppes of Asia through the Khyber Pass, and now by an Air India 747.

Gandhi stands in the maturity of this heritage and at the same time in the throes of India's birth into the modern world. For the eminent psychoanalyst, Dr. Erik Erikson, Gandhi represents and embodies a creative response to the crisis of man's maturity; and he sees in Gandhi's achievement a hope for mankind:

> . . . . to have faced mankind with nonviolence . . .
> marks the Mahatma's deed in 1919. In a period
> when proud statesmen could speak of a "war to
> end war;" when the superpolicemen of Versailles
> could bathe in the glory of a peace that would
> make "the world safe for democracy;" when the
> revolutionaries in Russia could entertain the be-
> lief that terror could initiate an eventual "wither-
> ing away of the State"—during that same period,
> one man in India confronted the world with the
> strong suggestion that a new political instrument,
> endowed with a new kind of religious fervor, may
> yet provide man with a choice.

> Erik Erikson, *Gandhi's Truth* (New York: W. W. Norton and
> Company, 1969).

Our study ends on this note of hope in the conviction that we still have much to learn about ourselves and about others who share this planet with us. We Americans, particularly, who have structured so much of our lives in terms of political and economic value, have much to learn of the symbolic meaning of life. This hope raises the possibility of achieving social unity without the dulling pall of conformity or the aggressive stimulation of success and competition. It may be that in a deepening sense of understanding that comes out of relationships with peoples who belong to other cultures, we may yet find occasion to survive.

SUGGESTED RESOURCE MATERIALS

CHAPTER I

Books

Basham, A.L. *The Wonder That Was India*. New York: Grove
 Press, 1959.

Forster, E.M. *A Passage to India*. New York: Harcourt Brace,
 1924.

Isaacs, Harold. *Scratches on Our Mind*. New York: John Day,
 1958. Also published as *Images of Asia*. New
 York: G.P. Putnam.

Rao, Raja. *The Serpent and the Rope*. New York: Pantheon,
 1963.

Schulberg, Lucille. *Historic India*. New York: Time-Life Publications, 1970.

Audio-Visuals

A good image of India is given in a 22 minute, black and
white film, *Barncaras*, produced by Michael Camerini. Illustrates the patterns of a day in that ancient city. Vivid and direct;
a good opener. (Available from Michael Camerini; 3935 Ply-
mouth Circle; Madison, Wisconsin 53705)

CHAPTER II

Books

Bettelheim, Charles. *India Independent,* trans. Anthony Caswell. New York: Monthly Review, 1971.

Lewis, John P. *Quiet Crisis in India.* New York: Doubleday, 1964.

Nair, Kusim. *Blossoms in the Dust.* New York: F.A. Praeger, 1962.

Rosen, George. *Democracy and Economic Change in India.* Berkeley: University of California Press, 1966.

CHAPTER III

Books

Brass, Paul. *Factional Politics in an Indian State: The Congress Party in Uttr Pradesh*. Berkeley: University of California Press, 1965.

Hardgrave, R. *India, Government and Politics in a Developing Nation*. Englewood Cliffs, New Jersey: Prentice Hall, 1970.

Harrison, Selig. *India: The Most Dangerous Decade*. Princeton: Princeton University Press, 1969.

Isaacs, Harold. *India's Ex-Untouchables*. New York: John Day, 1965.

Morris-Jones, W.P. *The Government and Politics of India*. London: Hutchinson University Library, 1964.

Palmer, N. *The Indian Political System*. Boston: Houghton Mifflin, 1961.

Smith, Donald, ed. *South Asian Politics and Religion*. Princeton: Princeton University Press, 1969.

CHAPTER IV

Books

Beals, Alan. *Gopalpur: A South Indian Village*. New York: Holt, Rinehart & Winston, 1965.

Lewis, Oscar. *Village Life in Northern India: Studies in a Delhi Village*. New York: Vintage Books, 1965.

Markandeya, Kamala. *Nectar in a Sieve*. New York: John Day, 1954.

Narayan, R.K. *The Bachelor of Arts*. Mysore: Indian Thought Publications, 1965.

_____. *The English Teacher*. Mysore: Indian Thought Publications, 1945. Also published as *Grateful to Life and Death.* East Lansing: Michigan State University Press, 1953.

Rao, Raja. *Kanthapura*. New York: New Directions, 1963.

Audio-Visuals

North Indian Village. 40 minutes, color film on the village. (Available from International Film Bureau; 3325 Michigan Avenue, Chicago, Illinois.)

Pather Panchali. Produced by Salyajit Ray. A feature film, delicate and beautiful, of Indian life.

Resources for Indian village study are being developed by Inter-Cultural Associates, Thompson, Connecticut. Study kits available based on Village Surveys prepared from 1961 Indian Census.

CHAPTER V

Books

Beteille, Andre. *Caste, Class, and Power*. Berkeley: University of California Press, 1965.

Brecher, Michael. *Nehru's Mantle*. London: Oxford University Press, 1966.

Rudolph, Susanne and Lloyd. *The Modernity of Tradition: Political Development in India*. Chicago: University of Chicago Press, 1967.

Silversten, Dagfinn. *When Caste Barriers Fall*. New York: Humanities Press, 1963.

Srinivas, M.N. *Social Change in Modern India*. Berkeley: University of California Press, 1969.

CHAPTER VI

Books

Clothey, Fred. "Skando-Shasti: A Festival in Tamil India," *History of Religions*, Vol. 8, no. 3, Feb. 1969.

Hudson, Dennis. "Two Citra Festivals in Madurai," Bardwell Smith, ed., *Asian Religions*, American Academy of Religion, 1971.

Singer, Milton, ed. *Krishna, Myths, Rite and Attitudes*. Chicato: Chicago University Press, 1969.

Singer, Milton and Bernard Cohn, eds. *Structure and Change in Indian Society*. Chicago: Aldine, 1968.

Singer, Milton, ed. *Traditional India: Structure and Change*. Philadelphia: American Folklore Society, 1959.

Audio-Visual

A number of films describing many of the ceremonies of an orthodox Brahmin community in Madras have been prepared by H. Daniel Smith and are available from Syracuse Film Rental Library, 1455 East Colvin Street, Syracuse, New York, 13201.

An excellent feature film on an Indian religious theme, produced by Satyajit Ray, is called *Devi*, the goddess. This film presents episodes from a festival, devotional singing, household ritual, and raises dramatically a question of religious truth and authority.

CHAPTER VII

Books

Bondurant, *Conquest of Violence.* Berkeley: University of California Press, 1965.

Erikson, Erik. *Gandhi's Truth.* New York: W.W. Norton, 1970.

Fischer, Louis. *The Life of Mahatma Gandhi.* Bombay: Bharatiya Vidya Bhavan, 1959.

Gandhi, Mohandas K. *An Autobiography: The Story of My Experiments with Truth,* trans. M. Desai, Boston: Beacon Press, 1957.

Narayan, R.K. *Waiting for the Mahatma.* East Lansing: Michigan State University Press, 1955.

Rao, Raja. *Kanthapura.* New York, New Directions, 1963.

INDEX